Snowy Owl Family

Animal Adventures

sequoia™
children's publishing

The long winter's snow is just beginning to melt away as Mother Snowy Owl scrapes a shallow nest on top of a very small hill. In spring it is cold on the Arctic tundra.

The ground is still wet, so Mother Owl lines the nest with moss and feathers. She settles into the nest, then she calls to Father Snowy Owl.

Father Snowy Owl must take good care of Mother Owl for the next few months. She has a very big job to do, and Father Owl will be around to help.

Mother Owl lays a glossy white, roundish egg in the nest and sits on top of it, sharing the warmth of her body with the egg. Father Owl brings a lemming for her to eat. He brings food to her so she doesn't have to leave the nest.

The next day, Mother Owl lays another white egg, and another two days after that, until there are eight eggs in the nest.

Mother Owl's feathers are mostly white. Her white feathers help Mother Owl blend in with the snow that makes up her environment.

The springtime wildflowers bloom brightly as Mother Owl sits patiently on the nest. She and Father Owl call to each other to keep in touch.

As the long spring days pass, Father Owl makes many flights to hunt for lemmings and hares. He flies swiftly and silently. Father Owl brings back meals he's caught in his sharp claws.

The lemmings that Father Owl catches are mouse-size animals that burrow beneath the snow in the late fall, winter, and early spring. They come out in the warmer months.

Finally the first tiny owlet hatches from the eggs laid by Mother Owl. This first little owl is called Baby Snowy, and he is covered with soft white down.

As soon as Snowy is able to eat, Father and Mother Owl feed him tender bits they have stored nearby. The next day, another owlet hatches. Ten days later, Snowy has seven brothers and sisters.

Owls eat insects, birds, and small mammals. But owls cannot digest bones and fur, so after they're done eating they bring up small pellets of undigested food.

A caribou wanders too close to the family's nest. Mother and Father Owl shrill "krick-krick, krick-krick" to drive him off. Snowy also tries his hardest to "krick-krick."

The caribou looks up from his grazing. When the caribou turns and wanders away from the nest, Father Owl calls out a loud "hoo-hoo."

Father Owl's call could probably be heard from very far away. His loud call let the caribou know that he has come too close to the nest.

Caribou visit the tundra during summertime.

Snowy and his owlet siblings grow bigger daily. Mother Owl no longer covers them in the nest. Mother Owl stands guard near the nest while Father Owl searches for a hare to feed the large family.

During the midsummer, when the Arctic nights are as light as day, Snowy steps out of the nest and spreads his wings.

Most owls are nocturnal, meaning they are active only at night when it's dark. But Snowy lives in the tundra where sometimes the sun shines all night.

Snowy strides down the small hill. He is the first owlet in the family to climb over the rocks and walk through all of the wildflowers near the nest. He sees a snow goose gliding above him.

Snowy is so happy, he hoots. Mother Owl and the owlets look over from the nest to make sure Snowy is safe.

One day, Snowy will be big enough to fly away from the nest and start his own family. He will always be smaller than his sisters, though. Male owls are smaller than female owls.

Snowy spends many hours exploring the tundra around the nest. Day by day, his brothers and sisters become explorers, too, as they grow old enough to leave the nest.